A MARY CHRISTMAS

a Mary Christmas

KATHLEEN M. CARROLL

FOREWORD BY ALFRED MCBRIDE, O.PRAEM.

Franciscan
MEDIA
Cincinnati, Ohio

Cover and book design by Mark Sullivan
Cover image © Chiff | Dreamstime.com

Scripture passages have been taken from *New Revised Standard Version Bible*, copyright
©1989 by the Division of Christian Education of the National Council of the
Churches of Christ in the U.S.A., and used by permission. All rights reserved.

LIBRARY OF CONGRESS CATALOGING-IN-PUBLICATION DATA
Carroll, Kathleen (Kathleen M.)
A Mary Christmas / Kathleen M. Carroll.
p. cm.
Includes bibliographical references (p.   ).
ISBN 978-1-61636-475-5 (alk. paper)
1. Rosary. 2. Franciscan crown. 3. Mary, Blessed Virgin, Saint—Devotion to.
4. Christmas—Meditations. I. Title.
BX2163.C34 2012
242'.74—dc23

2012020680

ISBN 978-1-61636-475-5

Copyright ©2012, Kathleen M. Carroll. All rights reserved.

Published by Franciscan Media
28 W. Liberty St.
Cincinnati, OH 45202
www.FranciscanMedia.org

Printed in the United States of America.

Printed on acid-free paper.

12 13 14 15 16   5 4 3 2 1

Contents

Foreword

> O Mother, how pure you are.
> You are untouched by sin.
> Yours was the privilege,
> to carry God within you.
> —from the *Liturgy of the Hours*

The secret of any good book about Mary is the faith and humanity of the author. Both talents appear in page after page of this inspiring tribute to Mary the mother of Jesus, true God and true man. Kathleen Carroll has created a portrait of Mary from the perspective of her seven joys, a medieval devotion begun by a Franciscan friar named James. This unique insight into Mary provides a much-needed spiritual uplift for our times when so much of the news is depressing.

It also awakens us to the whole purpose of Christian morality, which is the gift of joy. Jesus began the Sermon on the Mount with the Beatitudes—a word that means "joy." Our culture saddens us and tells us that Christian life will make us unhappy. Mary and Jesus urge us otherwise. The path of Mary and Jesus began with Christmas and songs like "Joy to the world." Their road finished with the Resurrection of Jesus and the Assumption of Mary, both occasions marked by songs peppered with "Alleluias." Joy frames our origin and destiny and weaves its way through the sorrows of our lives.

Kathleen Carroll leads us carefully through five joyful moments of Mary's experience with the conception and birth of Jesus. The author concludes with Mary's ecstasy over her two encounters with her Risen Son, first as he is fresh from the tomb and then her final union with Jesus in heaven. These are the seven joys of the world's most honored woman.

Some years ago, *Life* magazine featured Mary on its cover, and one comment in the accompanying article caught my attention. The text stated that one billion Hail Marys are prayed every day. Why? Because so many love our Blessed Mother, who gives us the joy in response to our hunger for it.

Throughout this book you will experience the difference between the culture's promise of happiness that relies on temporary satisfaction, thrills, and artificial stimulants. She introduces us to the sources of joy in union with God and the fellowship of the saints, above all with Mary. Divine joy calms us down, invites us to rest in God and in the heart of Mary. This spirituality of joy is infinitely more satisfying than the sadness we encounter every day in empty promises.

Since so many of the joys focus on the birth and youth of Jesus, the book's title, deservedly, is *A Mary Christmas*. Of course, it is a book for all seasons. If you want to be relieved from our culture's skeptical, hostile, and tiresome approach to faith, read this lovely Christmas present from Kathleen Carroll. Like all fine Catholic writers she knows how to present the timeless truths about Mary and Jesus with a feel for their humanity and awe at Christ's divinity and endless joy at Mary's remarkable faith.

Jesus felt that joy too. People praised his mother by saying, "Blessed is the womb that carried you and the breasts at which you nursed." He replied, "Blessed are those who hear the word of God and observe it" (Luke 11:27–28). Perhaps what Jesus was saying is this: "The only one who has heard God's word and really kept it is my mom." Amen.

Introduction

T H E   S E V E N   J O Y S   O F   M A R Y

At every Mass we assert that we wait in joyful hope for the coming of our Lord and Savior Jesus Christ. There is not a better time to reflect in joyful waiting than the quiet season of Advent, which comes before the celebration of Christmas. And there is no greater model of joy for us than Our Blessed Mother, Mary.

Though it might be more common to hear Mary described as the Mother of Sorrows, Scripture makes it clear that her life was also filled with great joys to temper those sorrows. Over time, it became popular to recall the joys of Mary during times of celebration and to remember her sorrows during times of mourning.

The tradition of the Seven Joys of Mary dates from the fifteenth century—as early as 1422. A novice Franciscan named James had a particular devotion to the Blessed Virgin that started when he was a child. Each day he would gather flowers from the field and weave them into a crown to place on a statue of Mary. When his superiors explained that his new duties as a friar would not allow him the leisure to continue this practice, young James was heartbroken. He thought he had found a home in the Order, but could not imagine having to sacrifice his daily devotion to Mary.

A solution presented itself in a vision. Mary instructed James to offer a garland of prayers instead of flowers, allowing him to continue his devotion even while doing his other work. Each group of Hail Marys was to be recited while meditating on one of the "joys" of Our Lady's life. According to the legend, James's novice master observed him at his devotions and saw an angel transforming the young man's prayers into flowers—beautiful roses separated by gold lilies—and weaving these into a crown for James's head. When the novice master asked James for an explanation, James related his own vision and how he had practiced the devotion.

From that time on this devotion, known as the Franciscan Crown rosary, has been popular throughout the Franciscan Order. The distinctive set of beads matching the prayer is often worn with a friar's habit and cord. Though the joys of Mary sometimes vary from list to list, the Franciscan Crown rosary includes:

The Annunciation: the moment when Mary learned from the lips of an angel that she would bear the Savior. This mystery teaches us how to receive "good news" into our lives—even when it may turn our lives upside down.

The Visitation: Mary's trip to support her cousin Elizabeth. This mystery inspires us to rise above our troubles by helping others with theirs.

The Nativity of Our Lord: the birth of Jesus in the most humble of circumstances. This mystery demonstrates the power in every-day occurrences.

The Adoration of the Magi: the mysterious visit from kings of the East. This mystery helps us appreciate that wisdom comes from unexpected places—even strangers, even other faith traditions.

The Finding of the Child Jesus in the Temple: the joyful family reunion after three days of panicked separation. This story reminds us to cherish our families and to find joy in the company of our loved ones.

The Appearance of the Risen Christ to his Mother: confirmation of all that Mary had known to be true about her divine Son. This mystery demonstrates how faith and patience are rewarded.

The Assumption and Coronation of Mary as Queen of Heaven: the fitting end to an extraordinary earthly life. Mary's journey from the Annunciation to the Assumption is a celebration of the results of that first, fateful "yes."

Other listings of the joys of Mary include the Ascension of the Lord and Pentecost. Within the Franciscan Order, this devotion has been promoted by St. Bonaventure, St. John Capistrano, and St. Bernardine of Siena.

Since the rosary by its nature is a meditation on the central mysteries in the lives of Jesus and Mary, it makes a good introduction to our preparation for Advent and Christmas. The unique flavor of these meditations is a focus on the joy with which Mary embraced these important moments in her life.

We will see that she did not passively deign to hear the angel Gabriel at the Annunciation or even grudgingly murmur her assent, but that she listened with joy and anticipation for that voice, received it with joy, and responded with a joy so profound that her song of praise, the Magnificat, is remembered to this day.

As we focus on our own waiting this Advent season, let us imitate that profound joy and see with new eyes the mysteries unfolding before us.

CHAPTER ONE

The Annunciation

In the sixth month the angel Gabriel was sent by God to a town in Galilee called Nazareth, to a virgin engaged to a man whose name was Joseph, of the house of David. The virgin's name was Mary. And he came to her and said, "Greetings favored one! The Lord is with you!" But she was much perplexed by his words and pondered what sort of greeting this might be. The angel said to her, "Do not be afraid, Mary, for you have found favor with God. And now, you will conceive in your womb and bear a son, and you will name him Jesus.

He will be great, and will be called the Son of the Most High, and the Lord God will give to him the throne of his ancestor David. He will reign over the house of Jacob forever, and of his kingdom there will be no end."

—Luke 1:26–33

*B*y the time of Gabriel's visit to Mary, the people of God had been awaiting their Messiah for millennia. From the story of the Fall in the Garden of Eden, through the trials of Noah and Abraham, through the captivity in Egypt and the journey to the Promised Land, under the rule of the Babylonians, the Persians, the Assyrians, and, now, the Romans, faithful Jews would ask, "How long, O Lord? How long?"

For one young girl in Palestine, though, there was not much wait, nor even enough time to get used to the idea that the fullness of time had at last come. Scripture tells us very little about Mary before the Annunciation, but tradition and the custom of the time suggest that she was thirteen or fourteen years old. We know that she was "betrothed" to Joseph, the carpenter—a situation similar to the engagement period we practice today, though one in which parents' preferences often carried more weight than those of the future spouses. We know that she lived in a culture that could be very dangerous, even lethal, for unmarried girls who became pregnant.

The most essential thing we know about Mary comes from the words addressed to her at the Annunciation. In his book *Angels of God: The Bible, the Church and the Heavenly Hosts,* Mike Aquilina makes this point clear:

> The appearance of Gabriel is a lot like the angelic announcements in the Old Testament. It might remind us especially of the announcement of Samson's birth: An angel comes to a woman to announce that she will bear a son who will save Israel. But there's a noticeable difference in tone.
>
> When Gabriel—who's not just an angel, remember, but an archangel—approached Mary, he started right off showing respect to her. She, the human being of flesh and blood, was greeted by an archangel as if she were in some way his superior.

That Old Testament angel also seemed concerned that Manoah's wife, the mother of Samson (Scripture does not even record her name), was going to botch things somehow. He salutes her as "barren" (where Gabriel calls Mary "full of grace"), and follows his announcement with a list of caveats: "Please be careful not to drink wine or similar drink, and not to eat anything unclean." Also, he instructs her, don't cut the child's hair. Then he mentions again (as though he thinks she might have forgotten) "you shall conceive and bear a son." The poor woman tells all of this to her husband who then proceeds to give the angel the third degree about the entire situation, and finally deigns to grant his permission that his wife be honored in such a manner (see Judges 13:2–24).

Gabriel, apparently full of confidence in Mary and joy at the wonderful news he is announcing, waxes poetic about how this child will save the world and rule the people of God forever. There is something in this difference that can tell us a lot about how the Incarnation changed what it means to be human. Aquilina suggests that the apostle Paul has a profound insight into this difference.

> I mean that the heir, as long as he is a child, is no better than a slave, though he is the owner of all the estate; but he is under guardians and trustees until the date set by the father. So with us; when we were children, we were slaves to the elemental spirits of the universe. But when the time had fully come, God sent his Son, born of woman, born under the law, to redeem those who were under the law, so that we might receive adoption as sons. (Galatians 4:1–5)

In the Old Testament, when we were struggling mightily to live up to the commandments of the Law of Moses (and failing equally mightily), the angels were like our nannies. They show up repeatedly, rescuing Isaac and Tobit, guarding the Israelites, making announcements designed to get us back on track, but clearly in charge of the circumstances, and frequently seeming a bit put-upon for having to deal with the likes of us. In the New Testament, through our life in Christ, we have been transformed from subpar creatures to sons and daughters of the Most High God, and the angels greet us with joy and deference.

Despite Gabriel's confidence, however, none of this was necessarily a foregone conclusion. After Gabriel makes his announcement, Mary has something to say. We know how the story ends, but at this moment she—this young, first-century teenaged girl—does not. When we encounter her story, it is sandwiched between the drama of the Old Testament and the astonishing ministry of Christ; when she experiences this moment it is—what? Between the innocence of childhood and the future she imagined with Joseph? Between her profound prayer life and the explanation she is going to have to offer to her parents, her neighbors, her fiancé? Between the cooking and the washing up?

She is the best of us, without doubt, but still one of us. And the future of the world rests on the answer she will give. St. Bernard captures the significance of this moment in a homily entitled "In Praise of the Virgin Mother":

> You have heard, O Virgin, that you will conceive and bear a son; you have heard that it will not be by man but by the Holy Spirit. The angel awaits an answer; it is time for him to return to God who sent him. We too are waiting, O Lady, for your word of compassion; the sentence of condemnation weighs heavily upon us.
>
> The price of our salvation is offered to you. We shall be set free at once if you consent. In the eternal Word of God we all came to be, and behold, we die. In your brief response we are to be remade in order to be recalled to life
>
> Tearful Adam with his sorrowing family begs this of you, O loving Virgin, in their exile from Paradise. Abraham begs it, David begs it. All the other holy patriarchs, your ancestors, ask it of you, as they dwell in the country of the shadow of death. This is what the whole earth waits for, prostrate at your feet. It is right in doing so, for on your

word depends comfort for the wretched, ransom for the captive, freedom for the condemned, indeed, salvation for all the sons of Adam, the whole of your race.

Answer quickly, O Virgin. Reply in haste to the angel, or rather through the angel to the Lord. Answer with a word, receive the Word of God. Speak your own word, conceive the divine Word. Breathe a passing word, embrace the eternal Word.[1]

It is a risk (in fact, nearly a certainty) that she will lose everything she loves—her future husband, her reputation, perhaps her family, perhaps even her life. Perhaps she even doubts what she is seeing and hearing—angelic visits are hardly everyday occurrences—and risks her sanity. Perhaps she imagines that this could even be a temptation—wouldn't it be prideful to imagine that angels salute you with such praise?—and risks her soul.

"Here am I, the servant of the Lord," she replies. "Let it be with me according to your word."

From that quiet yes has sprung every saint, every church, every act of kindness performed from Christian charity, our hope, and our salvation. But there is far more to come. Each moment of our lives is a question begging for an answer. The Word that was announced to Mary, that took flesh in her womb, is present to us today. It is announced to us in Scripture, in prayer, in the words and actions of others.

Recognizing the "Annunciations" in our lives takes practice. Most of us will not be disturbed in prayer because an archangel is knocking at the door. We must be open to believing that God might ask something special of us. Even more, we can take a cue from Mary's condition during that first Advent and expect it. Knowing that there must be some small way we can bring peace, or joy, or hope to someone else will prepare us to recognize the opportunities that come our way.

How do we respond to the Word of God that asks us to give him flesh in our words and actions? How do we consider the risks it asks of us—a few dollars? A few moments? A kind word? Are we willing to risk the embarrassment of being honest about our faith? Are we willing to risk a Sunday afternoon ball game or the ire of our angry-at-the-Church relatives? Are we willing to believe things we cannot prove? Are we willing to believe that God can do great things, even with the likes of us?

Christmas is a time that tests these questions. It is "announced" to us—we don't choose to celebrate it when the mood strikes us.

The question is upon us: How will we use this moment to bring Christ into the world?

In the thousand decisions we'll make this season, many will have no lasting impact. Whether you've decided that the icicle lights have one more year left in them or it's time to embrace the giant retro bulbs; whether you festoon the lawn with Sasquatch-sized inflatable snowmen or try to get those single candle lights to look Martha Stewart-perfect in each window; whether you choose ham or goose or paper or plastic, those results and all the time and effort you invested in achieving them will be fleeting, at best. But what we do with others can last a lifetime, or beyond.

History doesn't tell us what Mary wore the day of the Annunciation. We don't know what prayers she used, whether it was morning or evening, winter or summer. What we do know is that she was ready when the question came and recognized it for what it was. We know that she wasn't so caught up in her own designs that she dismissed this offer ("I can't think about this right now, I have a wedding to plan!"). And we know that, when her own course of life had been thwarted, she did not regret what she was leaving behind. She recognized this new path, full of sorrows though it would be, as a great gift and as the best life she could hope to live.

We will get such an offer this season. In fact, it might be waiting for our response right now. Is it to limit our holiday spending so we can create a celebration for a family that could not otherwise afford it? Is it to include that bitter cousin or weird uncle in our gatherings? Is it simply to smile through the traffic, the lines, the ten thousandth carol?

Each moment is an Annunciation, offering us the chance to bring Christ into the world through every word and action. This Christmas, embrace the risks and say yes.

CHAPTER TWO

The Visitation

In those days Mary set out and went with haste to a Judean town in the hill country, where she entered the house of Zechariah and greeted Elizabeth. When Elizabeth heard Mary's greeting, the child leapt in her womb. And Elizabeth was filled with the Holy Spirit and exclaimed with a loud cry, "Blessed are you among women, and blessed is the fruit of your womb. And why has this happened to me, that the mother of my Lord comes to me? For as soon as I heard the sound of your greeting, the child in my womb leapt for joy. And blessed is she who believed that there would be a fulfillment of what was spoken to her by the Lord."

—Luke 1:39-45

I have always been impressed by the way this story is told. In the midst of the great revelation she receives from the angel Gabriel, Mary learns this tidbit: "And now, your relative Elizabeth in her old age has also conceived a son; and this is the six month for her who was said to be barren" (Luke 1:36). This is nestled between the supernatural appearance of an archangel and agreeing to become the Mother of God Incarnate.

I imagine it might be like hearing my neighbor say, "The world is ending and you have been chosen to lead a colony of refugees to the moon. Did you know my Jimmy got into Brown? Also, you'll need to build the spaceship." I'm not sure how I'd react to such news, but I suspect my first thought would not be to go congratulate Jimmy.

That is the difference between me and Mary (yes, there are more than a few others). She does not run to her family to get help understanding the amazing news she has received. She does not run to Joseph to explain to him that things are about to get really strange. It may well be that she wants to see what's what with her cousin to gauge the truth of what the angel has told her, but from what we know of Mary, that doesn't quite ring true.

This woman who worries about the wine supply at a friend's wedding more than she worries about the repercussions of asking Jesus to perform an astonishing miracle, who comforts the disciples in the Upper Room while she herself has just witnessed her Son's execution simply doesn't spend a lot of time worrying about herself. She is always other-focused, always looking for ways to help.

And she doesn't merely respond graciously to requests sent her way. She doesn't wait for the announcement at the wedding at Cana that the wine has gone—she finds out about the problem and seeks a solution, perhaps even before the lack has a chance to dim the joy of the new bride and groom. She doesn't wait for her cousin to send for help or even make an offer and wait for an invitation. Wherever there's a need, she goes. And wherever she goes, she finds a way to help.

The Gospel According to Luke tells us the story of Elizabeth and Zechariah. Zechariah's experience with Gabriel provides a delightful contrast to Mary's:

In the days of King Herod of Judea, there was a priest named Zechariah, who belonged to the priestly order of Abijah. His wife was a descendant of Aaron, and her name was Elizabeth. Both of them were righteous before God, living blamelessly according to all the commandments and regulations of the Lord. But they had no children, because Elizabeth was barren, and both were getting on in years.

Once when he was serving as priest before God and his section was on duty, he was chosen by lot, according to the custom of the priesthood, to enter the sanctuary of the Lord and offer incense. Now at the time of the incense-offering, the whole assembly of the people was praying outside. Then there appeared to him an angel of the Lord, standing at the right side of the altar of incense. When Zechariah saw him, he was terrified; and fear overwhelmed him. But the angel said to him, "Do not be afraid, Zechariah, for your prayer has been heard. Your wife Elizabeth will bear you a son, and you will name him John. You will have joy and gladness, and many will rejoice at his birth, for he will be great in the sight of the Lord. He must never drink wine or strong drink; even before his birth he will be filled with the Holy Spirit. He will turn many of the people of Israel to the Lord their God. With the spirit and power of Elijah he will go before him, to turn the hearts of parents to their children, and the disobedient to the wisdom of the righteous, to make ready a people prepared for the Lord." Zechariah said to the angel, "How will I know that this is so? For I am an old man, and my wife is getting on in years." The angel replied, "I am Gabriel. I stand in the presence of God, and I have been sent to speak to you and to bring you this good news. But now, because you did not believe my words, which will be fulfilled in their time, you will become mute, unable to speak, until the day these things occur."

—Luke 1:5–20

If Gabriel's instructions about the wine and strong drink seem to echo some of the doubt we sensed in the announcement to Samson's mother, Zechariah loses no time in earning that doubt. This priest of the people, on one of the most privileged days of his life, in the great temple, right before the Holy of Holies, is visited with an angel sent to grant him the fondest wish of his life. His response? In modern parlance, I think it would be fair to describe it loosely as, "Prove it." Very satisfyingly, for those of us who bristle a bit at the insult to the archangel's dignity, Gabriel replies (again, loosely), "Shut up."

It's true that Mary asks a question of the angel as well, but hers does not express doubt. She does not say, "That's impossible. I'm a virgin." She asks instead, "How exactly is this going to work?" Her words indicate that she is actively a part of this situation, that she wants to know precisely what she's getting into. And for those who might irreverently suggest that the Incarnation was nothing more than an imaginative cover story for a young girl who found herself in trouble, she states clearly that this is not the case.

So, six months after Zechariah's experience when his wife Elizabeth is both "getting on in years" and now well into her pregnancy, Mary comes to visit. Elizabeth has been living in seclusion throughout her pregnancy and the one person available to reassure her and comfort her, her doubting husband, has been stricken dumb. (Whether Elizabeth found this a blessing or a curse, Scripture does not say.) But Mary's greeting brings her profound joy.

Neither Elizabeth nor Mary has been told about the child Elizabeth carries. Gabriel's revelation came to Zechariah, and he's not talking. But the unborn John leaps at Mary's greeting and Elizabeth is filled with the Holy Spirit. She cries out the words that every generation has uttered since, "Blessed are you among women, and blessed is the fruit of your womb!" And, as if to confirm Mary's faith in the words of the angel, Elizabeth says, "And blessed is she who believed that there would be a fulfillment of what was spoken to her by the Lord."

What follows next is one of the greatest songs of praise in all of Scripture. They are they only recorded words spoken by Mary during her pregnancy and they are stilled prayed by the Church every day in the Liturgy of the Hours. It is her Magnificat:

And Mary said,
"My soul magnifies the Lord,
and my spirit rejoices in God my Savior,
for he has looked with favor on the lowliness of his
    servant.
Surely, from now on all generations will call me blessed;
for the Mighty One has done great things for me,
and holy is his name.
His mercy is for those who fear him
from generation to generation.

He has shown strength with his arm;
he has scattered the proud in the thoughts of their hearts.
He has brought down the powerful from their thrones,
and lifted up the lowly;
he has filled the hungry with good things,
and sent the rich away empty.
He has helped his servant Israel,
in remembrance of his mercy,
according to the promise he made to our ancestors,
to Abraham and to his descendants forever."

—Luke 1: 46–55

This is one of the clearest portraits of Mary Scripture gives us. Burdened with a tremendous secret of her own, she thinks only of how she can help others. Faced with an uncertain future and great danger, she can only praise God.

Christmas is full of our own visitations. We see friends and family that we might not see at any other time of year. We visit with our own ghosts of Christmas past when we tell the origin story of each shiny star or construction paper chain we hang on the tree. We remember the best and worst holidays of our childhoods and vow to do better for the children in our lives.

It can be tempting to use our busyness as an excuse to ignore the problems of others ("I can't volunteer at the parish center, I've got a house to decorate!"). And it can be even more tempting to let our own problems become the dominant feature in our mental landscape. On top of the usual bills and obligations, the holidays often bring extra expenses, more tasks, and a whole host of expectations. Will the neighbors think we're pagans if we don't hang the lights this year? Does this gift say, "I'm practical," or, "I'm cheap"? What will she think of me if she knows I've forgotten her size, again?

Mary's example demonstrates a boundless confidence. She seems to have no doubt that God is in charge of her life and will take care of her. Her only concern is for those who lack that confidence, who need some tangible sign that they are cared for as well.

Do we have that confidence? Do we face the approaching season obsessing over how it will all get done? Or do we reflect that, somehow, it has all always gotten done? Do we give gifts that will make us look good? Or do we try to find what our loved ones really need? Do we feel so overwhelmed by the needs of others that we ignore invitations and requests for help? Or do we actively seek out the needs of others and find a way to help?

We can't give what we don't have. But if we consider all that God has done for us in the past, we might begin to understand that there is nothing we haven't been given. And once we know we have it all, it's only natural to want to share that with others.

This Christmas, bring that little bit of Jesus you carry in your heart wherever he directs you. Find out what's needed, and find a way to help.

CHAPTER THREE

The Nativity of Our Lord

In that region there were shepherds living in the fields, keeping watch over their flock by night. Then an angel of the Lord stood before them, and the glory of the Lord shone around them, and they were terrified. But the angel said to them, "Do not be afraid; for see—I am bringing you good news of great joy for all the people: to you is born this day in the city of David a Savior, who is the Messiah, the Lord. This will be a sign for you: you will find a child wrapped in bands of cloth and lying in a manger." And suddenly there was with the angel a multitude of the heavenly host, praising God and saying,

"Glory to God in the highest heaven,
and on earth peace among those whom he favors!"

When the angels had left them and gone into heaven, the shepherds said to one another, "Let us go now to Bethlehem and see this thing that has taken place, which the Lord has made known to us." So they went with haste and found Mary and Joseph, and the child lying in the manger. When they saw this, they made known what had been told them about this child; and all who heard it were amazed at what the shepherds told them. But Mary treasured all these words and pondered them in her heart. The shepherds returned, glorifying and praising God for all they had heard and seen, as it had been told them.

—Luke 2:8–20

*W*hen I first heard my mother tell me, "God is no respecter of persons," I had no idea what she was talking about. Even to my young mind it seemed that God was, if anything, excessively respectful of persons, giving us mere humans more dignity than we could be said to deserve. And though Mom would often quote other texts that turned out to be not so scriptural—"God helps those who help themselves," "Waste not, want not," "Don't load up on the bread"—it turns out she was right on with the "respecter of persons" business. It just took a few years for me to understand what that meant.

When Peter uttered these words he was explaining that God did not show favoritism to those who were wealthy or well-bred, not even to the chosen people, "but in every nation anyone who fears him and does what is right is acceptable to him" (Acts 10:35).

The story of the Nativity is a good illustration of this.

The angels do not announce the birth of the Savior to the rulers of every land, they tell the closest people they can find—even if they're humble shepherds. Mary doesn't wrap her newborn babe in purple or silk, she swaddles him with what's available—even if it's only strips of cloth. And she doesn't demand a golden crib for her Son, she makes do with what's handy—even if it's a hay-filled manger.

The Gospels are full of such examples. Jesus uses parables of everyday life to give his listeners some sense of what the kingdom of heaven is like. It's like a mustard seed, or leaven, or a lost coin. He heals people with a word, a touch, or even a bit of mud. He turns water into wine, and wine into blood.

As the fullest expression of God's revelation, Jesus himself is how God communicates to us. Imagine that the creator of heaven and earth loves you so much that he wants to leave heaven behind to become human like you, to share in your joys and your trials, to walk this same earth, breathe this same air. Imagine that, even as he wants to share your humanity, he offers you a share in his divinity, a share in his exuberant ecstasy, a place in his kingdom, a view of eternity. Imagine that he would die just to convince you that this is true.

Of course, nothing about the Incarnation is the least bit imaginable and, even with two thousand years to get used to the idea, we still have trouble believing it. Most of the Old Testament and most of our childhood teaches us that things that are holy are not like us. Indeed, the Hebrew word for *holy* means "set apart."

Things that are holy are set apart for God's use; the chosen people are set apart for God's service. We learn that we don't wear our church clothes to play, rosaries aren't jewelry, and we don't say "Jesus" unless we're talking to him or about him. The idea that things become more holy the further from us they get seems to make a lot of sense. We're all broken and damaged humans and we're not eager to besmirch the sanctity of our Lord by mucking about in his presence with our meager selves.

As it happens, the Lord's sanctity is not as fragile as we might imagine. Sin is the damage we do to our relationship with God, not some cosmic schmutz we'll get all over him if we get too close. Could we ever hurt God, though? Could he allow himself to be that vulnerable? He could and he did, and we put our very best efforts into it. We got our most morally upright humans involved—first-century Jews who lived and breathed the Law of Moses. Their job was to explain that Jesus was a blasphemer, an impostor, a man whose ego threatened the survival of all Israel.

Then we recruited some Romans, who had been perfecting some very creative torture techniques for just such an occasion, to strip him, taunt him, parade him through the streets as an object of scorn, and execute him in a manner we have yet to surpass in horror. Those of us who were his friends abandoned him, denied even knowing him. If you had personally been on the committee charged with perpetrating the most cruel and blasphemous assault possible, I suspect you could not have come up with anything worse.

Still, unbelievably still, he loves us, longs to be with us. The Scriptures resound with God's longing for us:

> Though your sins are like scarlet,
>   they shall be like snow;
> though they are red like crimson,
>   they shall become like wool. (Isaiah 1:18)

> Return to me, says the LORD of hosts, and I will return to
>   you. (Zechariah 1:3)

> The LORD waits to be gracious to you;
>   therefore he will rise up to show mercy to you. (Isaiah
>   30:18)

> Do not fear, for you will not be ashamed;
>   do not be discouraged, for you will not suffer disgrace;

for you will forget the shame of your youth,
   and the disgrace of your widowhood you will
   remember no more.
For your Maker is your husband,
   the LORD of hosts is his name;
the Holy One of Israel is your Redeemer,
   the God of the whole earth he is called.
For the LORD has called you
   like a wife forsaken and grieved in spirit,
like the wife of a man's youth when she is cast off,
   says your God.
For a brief moment I abandoned you,
   but with great compassion I will gather you.
In overflowing wrath for a moment
   I hid my face from you,
but with everlasting love I will have compassion on you,
   says the LORD, your Redeemer. (Isaiah 54:4–8)

But Zion said, "The LORD has forsaken me,
   my LORD has forgotten me."
Can a woman forget her nursing child,
   or show no compassion for the child of her womb?

Even these may forget,
> yet I will not forget you. (Isaiah 49:14–15)

I ask not only on behalf of these, but also on behalf of those who will believe in me through their word, that they may all be one. As you, Father, are in me and I am in you, may they also be in us, so that the world may believe that you have sent me. The glory that you have given me I have given them, so that they may be one, as we are one, I in them and you in me, that they may become completely one, so that the world may know that you have sent me and have loved them even as you have loved me. Father, I desire that those also, whom you have given me, may be with me where I am, to see my glory, which you have given me because you loved me before the foundation of the world. (John 17:20–24)

The Gospel according to John tells us that "God is love," and this is always the default setting when it comes to our creator. He does not wait for us to become perfect or event to repent, but calls us constantly, even while we're struggling with our faults or refusing to acknowledge them altogether. God takes what is at hand and finds the good in it. He takes what is humble and elevates it to a higher purpose.

As anyone who has children in their lives can attest, this is not a matter of turning a blind eye to faults or wishful thinking. Young people tend to live up to—or down to—our expectations of them. Children who know they are loved become loving; those who are neglected or abused often become neglectful or abusive themselves. Those who are told they are smart and beautiful tend to take care of their studies and their appearance; those who are told they are ugly and stupid have little incentive to try.

Even material things demonstrate this result. It's not hard to tell the difference between a house that is loved and one that is not, or the yard of an attentive gardener from that of someone who takes no interest. We frame our family photos, repeatedly dust treasured keepsakes, maintain memory books of handmade cards, ticket stubs, and autographs. People and things blossom with love.

Many people have difficulty rising to the challenges of the Christmas season (or the Christian life in general) because they feel a lack of love. Whether due to one of the countless tragedies of childhood, a failed friendship, a marriage ended by death or divorce, this perceived deficit can make it hard to participate in the season of giving with enthusiasm. You can't give away what you don't have.

Our faith has the remedy. Whatever failings our parents, siblings, or partners may have had, we have an alternate source for the love we so desperately crave. The Nativity is a concrete demonstration of God's love for us—a love that, given the chance, will fill every need and exceed every expectation. This love can be impossible to express in human terms, but it has a way of supplying just what we need, just when we need it. If we can look beyond our circumstances and beyond the merely material, we can catch a glimpse of it.

Christmas is the perfect time to watch this principle in action. The most cherished gifts are rarely the most expensive, but often those that are more creative or that best express the unique relationship of the giver and the recipient. The most precious ornament on the tree might not be the biggest and shiniest, but might be a kindergartner's glitter experiment or a tarnished bell that was Grandma's.

The temptation to prepare for the new year by shedding the old and embracing the new can make us overlook the value in what's right in front of us. It's a good opportunity to think twice before casting off items that may still have some use. It's also a chance to recognize that what may have lost its luster for us might still be appreciated by someone new. Those items you think you might give to charity could find their way to someone else's tree if you act early enough.

This Christmas, take a second look at the items—and the people—for which you've lost appreciation. Your reevaluation might give them a new lease on life.

CHAPTER FOUR

The Adoration of the Magi

In the time of King Herod, after Jesus was born in Bethlehem of Judea, wise men from the East came to Jerusalem, asking, "Where is the child who has been born king of the Jews? For we observed his star at its rising, and have come to pay him homage." When King Herod heard this, he was frightened, and all Jerusalem with him; and calling together all the chief priests and scribes of the people, he inquired of them where the Messiah was to be born. They told him, "In Bethlehem of Judea; for so it has been written by the prophet:

'And you, Bethlehem, in the land of Judah,
are by no means least among the rulers of Judah;
for from you shall come a ruler who is to shepherd my
people Israel.'"

Then Herod secretly called for the wise men and learned from them the exact time when the star had appeared. Then he sent them to Bethlehem, saying, "Go and search diligently for the child; and when you have found him, bring me word so that I may also go and pay him homage."

When they had heard the king, they set out; and there, ahead of them, went the star that they had seen at its rising, until it stopped over the place where the child was. When they saw that the star had stopped, they were overwhelmed with joy. On entering the house, they saw the child with Mary his mother; and they knelt down and paid him homage. Then, opening their treasure chests, they offered him gifts of gold, frankincense, and myrrh. And having been warned in a dream not to return to Herod, they left for their own country by another road.

—Matthew 2:1–12

*O*ne reason Catholics turn to Mary for guidance is that she unerringly points us to her Son. Though she has risked everything to bring Jesus into the world, Mary is not interested in glory for herself. This episode is listed among the joys of Mary because it is a rare occasion when her Son receives the treatment due him.

Scripture tells us very little about these wise men from the East, but our tradition is rich with legends about them. Though their three gifts are mentioned, Matthew mentions no names. He does not even say that there were three wise men—this tradition developed from an assumption that three gifts must imply three givers.

The word *magi* seems to have originated in Persia, with the hereditary priesthood that Darius the Great established as the state religion. In fact, one of the sources of Daniel's troubles (see the book of Daniel) was the eminence he gained under the rulers Nebuchadnezzar, Darius the Mede, and Cyrus the Persian. The prophet's gift of interpreting dreams infringed on the duties of the Magi, who sought his downfall. Our word *magic* comes from this same origin and carries with it the early significance of divination, dream interpretation, and astrology.

These astrologers follow a star to Bethlehem and leave according to instructions they receive in a dream. Clearly they not only excel at these traditional skills but also have confidence enough in their abilities to follow these signs and dreams, even across great distances, even when it may seem contrary to sensible behavior.

The gifts they bring, though familiar by tradition, seem strange choices for an infant. Whenever I read this account, it calls to mind a favorite exchange from *A Charlie Brown Christmas*:

> **Lucy Van Pelt**: I know how you feel about all this Christmas business, getting depressed and all that. It happens to me every year. I never get what I really want. I always get a lot of stupid toys or a bicycle or clothes or something like that.
> **Charlie Brown**: What is it you want?
> **Lucy Van Pelt**: Real estate.

Though gold could be argued to be eternally useful, frankincense and myrrh are another matter. What is the meaning behind these choices?

Once again, we come to the heart of why this event was cherished by Mary. These gifts are prophetic, and each corresponds to a hidden facet of Jesus's identity.

Gold has always been an emblem of royalty. It is rare and difficult to mine and purify, making it valuable. It has a universality that other means of exchange lack—locally minted coins, say, or the salt used by the Roman army. The gift of gold is a salute to Christ's royalty (the wise men describe him as "king of the Jews") and the universal scope of his rule.

Frankincense was the incense offered to God at the temple— the same incense Zechariah was burning when he was visited by the angel. Though it, too, was a valuable commodity, it was more prized for this exclusive use.

> When you make incense according to this composition, you shall not make it for yourselves; it shall be regarded by you as holy to the LORD. Whoever makes any like it to use as perfume shall be cut off from the people. (Exodus 30:37–38)

Its presence here symbolizes the divinity of Christ (frankincense was offered only to God) and his priesthood (only the priest was allowed to offer it).

Myrrh is mentioned in the Talmud as another ingredient of the incense offered in temple worship, but it does not appear in the "recipe" given by the Lord in Exodus. It was part of the holy anointing oil described in the same chapter of Exodus (verses 23–33):

> The LORD spoke to Moses: Take the finest spices: of liquid myrrh five hundred shekels, and of sweet-smelling cinnamon half as much, that is, two hundred fifty, and two hundred fifty of aromatic cane, and five hundred of cassia—measured by the sanctuary shekel—and a hin of olive oil; and you shall make of these a sacred anointing oil blended as by the perfumer; it shall be a holy anointing oil. With it you shall anoint the tent of meeting and the ark of the covenant, and the table and all its utensils, and the lampstand and its utensils, and the altar of incense, and the altar of burnt offering with all its utensils, and the basin with its stand; you shall consecrate them, so that they may be most holy; whatever touches them will become holy. You shall anoint Aaron and his sons, and consecrate them, in order that they may serve me as priests. You shall say to the Israelites, "This shall be my holy anointing oil throughout your generations. It shall

not be used in any ordinary anointing of the body, and you shall make no other like it in composition; it is holy, and it shall be holy to you. Whoever compounds any like it or whoever puts any of it on an unqualified person shall be cut off from the people."

So, we might read this gift of myrrh as another tribute to Jesus's holiness. However, myrrh had other uses as well. It was used as a cure-all throughout Ancient Greece and the Roman Empire, and made into a salve that relieved pain when applied to the skin. If these uses had an air of foreboding, myrrh's most common use was to anoint the dead.

Whether Mary had any sense of the trials that lay ahead for her Son is unclear—she had yet to visit the temple and hear the warning of Simeon, "a sword will pierce your own soul too." And these dream interpreting prognosticators from the East belonged to a different faith altogether. Could they have foreseen the manner in which God would redeem his people, when the greatest scholars of Judaism expected something very different?

Most Scripture scholars interpret the gifts of the Magi as tributes to Jesus's roles as king, priest, and Savior. Mary knew her Son was special; it certainly didn't take the opinion of outsiders to convince her. But she rejoices in the honor paid her Son, just as she cherishes our own offerings to him. Though God does not "need" our worship any more than an infant "needs" exotic spices, it is still a righteous and worthwhile practice. Prayer doesn't change God, as the old saying goes. But if we let it, it just might change us.

Christmas is a holy day of obligation for Catholics. Behind Easter, it is the most solemn celebration of the year. While Mass was once *the* thing you did for Christmas, it sometimes gets shoehorned between the morning gift frenzy and dinner at Grandma's as some trifling inconvenience. Some Protestant churches have recently adopted the fashion of being closed altogether for Christmas, so that staff and members can spend the day with family. Somehow we've managed to hold on to the components of this Christmas story while missing the point altogether.

There is some gift-giving here, but they are gifts given to *Jesus*. Joseph and Mary aren't exchanging baubles or finding treats for the animals in the stable. And those gifts aren't given to Jesus because he's a baby (and Christmas is all about the children after all), but because he's *Jesus*—the newborn king, the Messiah, the Savior of the world. And they aren't given to him because they're things he might like to play with; they are symbols of the worship we are called to offer him at Mass.

There is some visiting here, too. But it's not a jaunt across town to see Memaw and Pop-Pop and the cousins. The Magi travel from afar to see *Jesus*.

This Christmas, follow the example of the wise men and make Jesus the center of your attention.

CHAPTER FIVE

The Finding of the Child Jesus in the Temple

Now every year his parents went to Jerusalem for the festival of the Passover. And when he was twelve years old, they went up as usual for the festival. When the festival was ended and they started to return, the boy Jesus stayed behind in Jerusalem, but his parents did not know it. Assuming that he was in the group of travelers, they went a day's journey. Then they started to look for him among their relatives and friends. When they did not find him, they returned to Jerusalem to search for him. After three days they found him in the temple, sitting among the teachers, listening to them and asking them questions. And all who heard him were amazed at his understanding and his answers. When his parents saw him they were astonished; and his mother said to him, "Child, why have you treated us like this? Look, your father and I have been searching for you in great anxiety." He said to them, "Why were you searching for me? Did you not know that

I must be in my Father's house?" But they did not understand what he said to them. Then he went down with them and came to Nazareth, and was obedient to them. His mother treasured all these things in her heart. And Jesus increased in wisdom and in years, and in divine and human favor.

—Luke 2:41–52

A catechist friend of mine has the perfect explanation for the silence of Scripture on Jesus's formative years: He was grounded. After the episode of the finding in the temple, I can believe it.

This story was a great inspiration to me in the midst of the challenges of child rearing. Whenever I was tempted to believe that Mary could be the perfect mother only because she had the perfect Son, it set me straight. What other challenges did she have to face that I was spared?

Sure, there was that whole I'm-unmarried-and-pregnant-but-I-didn't-do-anything-wrong conversation she must have had with her friends and family (to say nothing of her betrothed). And I suppose that traveling to Bethlehem while nine months along might not have been too pleasant, even if she did have the "benefit" of a donkey to ride. Delivering a child in a barn was probably no picnic, either. Yes, by the time I got to Day One, Mary had outparented me by an unbridgeable margin.

This is the one "typical" episode we see of Jesus's childhood. It wasn't the first time the family had traveled to Jerusalem; they went every year. They traveled with a group of friends and relatives large enough that it was possible to walk all day long and not miss a twelve-year-old boy.

These are people whose lives revolve around their faith. They think nothing of making a regular trek from Nazareth to Jerusalem—on foot. The distance was about sixty-five miles, but it was common for Jews to take a detour around Samaria (you'll remember the parable of the Good Samaritan), adding to the distance. Their friends and family are all like-minded. The annual trip to Jerusalem (Joseph would have gone three times a year) would have been arduous, expensive, even dangerous. Yet they embrace it without complaint. The distraction of so many friends along the journey even seems to give the impression that they were enjoying themselves.

And this boy of theirs, this twelve-year-old boy, is so comfortable at the temple that he apparently doesn't notice when everyone else leaves. He's still there, days later, talking with the most learned religious men of his people and dazzling them with his insight.

When I compare these folks to me, well, there's no comparison. I live so close to my parish church that I can wake up when the Mass bells ring and still make it there on time with a full three minutes of grumbling before I get out of bed. If I miss the 8 AM, it's about a ten-minute drive to the cathedral for an early evening Mass. But, ugh, ten minutes! And there could be traffic! Or something on TV.

I suppose I hardly need to say that the children rarely bother me to get to church early or beg me to take them to St. Peter's Basilica for the Easter service.

This story reminds me that there are no excuses for missing Mass, nor should anyone be looking for any. For those who contend that they don't need "to go to some church to talk to God," you might want to tell that to Mary and Joseph who, quite literally, had Jesus in their backyard. They still took him to the temple when he was eight days old and made the trek to Jerusalem every year. Jesus would one day change all the rules but, as they say of a good artist, you have to know the rules before you can break them.

But what of this seeming disobedience of Jesus? Surely he could not have meant to cause his parents such distress.

There comes a time in all our lives when we discover (sometimes to our complete surprise) that not everyone agrees on the correct course of behavior. We teach our children to share, but would be none too pleased if they gave away that expensive new video game system. We teach them to be peaceable and then shout, "Mow 'em down!" at a football game. We want them to believe that everyone is equal, but we still think they shouldn't play with certain kids who just have trouble written all over them.

Church history is rich with stories of great saints who had to leave their families behind in order to pursue the life to which God called them. Francis of Assisi famously stripped bare in the public square in front of the bishop and the rest of the town (if they were not gathered there at first, word spread quickly). He surrendered his clothes as the property of his father, Pietro Bernardone, and announced, "Henceforth I have no father but my Father in heaven." As far as history records, he never spoke to his father again.

Clare of Assisi followed his example, sneaking out of her family's home one Palm Sunday night and making her way to Francis and his brothers. When her brothers came to seize her and drag her home, she revealed her shaved head and her resolve to stay. Her disappointed family did not rejoice that they had gained a saint; they mourned that they had lost a daughter.

Elizabeth Ann Seton, founder of the Sisters of Charity and a pioneer in Catholic education in the United States, faced smilar prejudice. Though raised in the Episcopal denomination, she found herself wrestling with the "big questions" of life when her husband died, leaving her the destitute mother of five small children. She found material and spiritual help from her husband's family and eventually converted to their Catholic faith. This was unpopular socially (anti-Catholic laws had only recently been repealed) and met with great resistance from her family. Several years later, when she received permission to found her new order, she actually had to step over one of her sons (who had blocked the entrance in protest) in order to take the veil.

Even for Mary and Joseph, whom no one would accuse of hypocrisy, there are conflicts: between faith and family, between one career and another, between obeying God and obeying your parents (whom God commands you to obey). Every parent will recognize their anxiety in searching for their Son, and resonate with Mary's chastisement of Jesus. Just so, every young person will recognize Jesus's amazement that there could be any confusion about where he would be or what he would be doing. I know I was firmly in Jesus's camp when I was younger and then staunchly defended Mary once I had children of my own.

Christmas is a time when many of these conflicts heat up. We may have friends and family members that no longer practice their faith, have a different faith altogether, or no faith at all. If we invite them to join us for Mass, are we extending an olive branch or fueling the fire with gasoline?

As in all things, Jesus is our role model. He put faith ahead of family (even *his* family!) and was willing to suffer the unpleasant consequences. His example becomes even bolder in his public ministry. He defies convention by healing on the Sabbath. He clashes repeatedly with the religious authorities, challenging their teaching, mocking their hypocrisy. When this conflict threatens his life, he willingly lays it down, leaving his Mother and closest friends to contemplate life without him.

We know that he was no callous idealist so bent on his own way of doing things that he disregarded the feelings of others. The Gospels reveal many intimate moments Jesus shared with his friends. Yet, even the fierce love he bore them had to be set aside when it conflicted with his mission.

This Christmas, embrace your faith, even if it means leaving friends and family behind. Just be sure to leave a note.

CHAPTER SIX

The Appearance of the Risen Christ to His Mother

The tradition of the risen Jesus appearing to his mother had a long history, and appeared as early as in the writings of St. Ambrose in the fourth century. I further discovered that the Ignatian expert Philip Endean, S.J., in an article in *The Way*, identified Ludolf of Saxony's *Vita Christi (Life of Christ)* as a source of the tradition of the risen Jesus appearing to his mother, a source which was known to Ignatius and was used by him when writing his Spiritual Exercises…. True enough, Ludolf did give a reference to Ambrose. Unfortunately it was not quite accurate, and correcting it took further research.

We know that during his convalescence from operations following his battle injury at Pamplona, the bored Ignatius had access to Ludolf's four-volume *Life of Christ* and in this the Cistercian writer devoted a whole chapter to enquiring, "How the Lord Jesus appeared to his Mother." He describes how the women going to the tomb to anoint the body of Jesus did so with his mother's permission. He later observed that it seemed surprising that Mary did not go with the women. Repeating Augustine, he suggested as possible reasons for this that it would have been too much for her and that out of concern for her, John, to whom she had been entrusted by Jesus, would not permit her to go, adding finally that "the blessed Virgin knew that he was not there, but had risen immortal and incorruptible." For "while our Lady was praying and gently weeping, suddenly the Lord Jesus came" and appeared to his mother. She embraced him, 'her mourning transformed into happiness," and sharing their joy they sat and conversed about what had happened to him and what he had been doing since, while she reassured herself that his sufferings were really over. It was true, Ludolf continued, that the gospel said nothing about this appearance of Jesus to his mother before anyone else, but it was fitting and was a pious belief more fully described in "a certain legend about the resurrection." Moreover, the Roman Church celebrated it by a station at St Mary Major's, and Ambrose himself gave witness to it. Finally, Ludolf observed, unlike Jesus' other Easter appearances, which were aimed at proving his resurrection from the dead, "he appeared first of all to his Virgin Mother, not to prove his resurrection but to delight her at the sight of him."[2]

*A*long with the seven joys of Mary we celebrate in this book, tradition records seven sorrows of Mary:

The Prophecy of Simeon: When Mary and Joseph present Jesus at the temple according to the requirements of the Law of Moses, this holy man recognizes that this infant is the promised savior. He also foresees the pain Mary will suffer and prophetically warns, "a sword will pierce your own soul, too."

The Flight Into Egypt: An angel of the Lord appears in a dream, warning Joseph to take Mary and the baby away from the reach of Herod, who has ordered the massacre of every male child under two years old.

The Loss of Jesus in the Temple: We have considered Mary's joy at finding Jesus, but what must her suffering have been like those three days?

Mary Meets Jesus on the Way to the Cross: When Jesus meets the women of Jerusalem, bewildered and bemoaning his fate, he tells them not to weep for him, but for themselves and their children.

Jesus Dies on the Cross: While most of his disciples had abandoned him, Mary stands at the foot of the cross, suffering with her Son to the very end.

Mary Receives the Dead Body of Her Son: Beautifully memorialized in Michelangelo's *Pieta*, Mary cradles her Son at the end of his life just as she did at the beginning.

Jesus Is Laid in the Tomb: Mary buries her Son in a tomb donated by Joseph of Arimathea. With the Sabbath approaching, there is not enough time to anoint the body properly.

Of the seven greatest heartbreaks in Mary's life, four occurred in the last twenty-four hours of Jesus's life, and her state at that time must have reminded her of a fifth—those three days in Jerusalem when she searched frantically for her young Son. Now, though, he had gone where she could not follow; she had no hope of finding him and bringing him home again.

What must it have meant to her to see him again? We do not know how much she knew of her Son's mission. She was faithful, yes, and sinless, but did she know she would see him again this side of heaven?

Scripture does not mention Mary by name among those to whom the Risen Christ appeared. She could certainly have been counted among "the women who had come with him from Galilee" whom Luke mentions (23:55), or the "many other women who had come up with him to Jerusalem" mentioned by Mark (15:41). It could have seemed so obvious to the Gospel writers that Jesus's Mother would have been by his side at every opportunity that they thought it superfluous to mention her by name. But the theory offered by St. Ambrose and St. Ignatius of Loyola is even more intriguing.

If Mary did not accompany those women to anoint Jesus's body at the tomb, why not? In wrestling with this question, St. Augustine suggests that she may have been overwhelmed by grief, but Augustine himself is clearly no expert on what causes grief to mothers (just ask his long-suffering mother, St. Monica). How could a woman be strong enough to accompany her Son through the torture and humiliation of his last hours, and yet be unable to perform a last service for him when he is laid to rest?

When Ignatius considered the venerable tradition that Jesus appeared to Mary before all others, he did not dismiss it as wishful thinking. Nor did he seem troubled by the omission of the tale from the Gospel accounts. If a woman so used to miracles could routinely accept them and ponder the mystery "in her heart," why would anyone have heard about her experience? Just as she tells us nothing about those quiet eighteen years of Jesus's young adulthood, some things appear to be better kept between Mother and Son.

The most persuasive line from Ignatius—the one that convinces me—is the idea that, though Jesus appeared to many after the Resurrection to prove that he had conquered sin and death, Mary needed no proof. She just needed to see him. She simply missed her Son. And this Son, who had already witnessed the pain he could cause his Mother by a few days' absence, wouldn't deny her that reward for her faith, her patience, her perseverance. What son would?

For those who have lost loved ones—which is all of us, eventually—Christmas can be a time of bittersweet memories. Our happiest childhood remembrances are clouded when that first, original Santa is gone and we must wearily and clumsily take his place. Recollections of just last year can be painful when we lose sight of who's with us, to remember who isn't.

Mary, too, lost those closest to her. For her, it wasn't the more common passing of parents that summed her loss, nor her widowhood, nor even that greatest heartbreak of all, the death of a child. She weathered all these losses. Once Jesus had left her for good, she was so utterly alone that she depended on one of her Son's friends—St. John—for support. Few of us will be tested by such grief.

Still, Scripture never records tears from Mary. Even Jesus wept when his friend Lazarus died, but Mary confronts challenging moments with faith, joyful moments with song, and life's darkest moments with waiting, watching, and prayer.

When Gabriel looks for her at the Annunciation, he finds her in prayer. When Elizabeth praises her, she responds with prayer and praise. There can be no doubt that she prayed for those three anxious days when Jesus stayed behind at the temple. When the Holy Spirit descended upon the disciples in the Upper Room at Pentecost, Mary was there among them, praying. Can there be any doubt that she prayed at the foot of the cross and for those three days Jesus laid in the tomb?

Prayer is best thought of as a gift of our faith, rather than a requirement of it. We will all experience loss, even abandonment, at some point in our lives. But we know that God is there, waiting to help us make sense of it all, to come through the fire better and stronger than we were before.

At the Last Supper, Jesus warns his disciples that they will face trials and persecutions, but points out that we should not expect to avoid suffering when our master has embraced it. No matter what we face, it's not hard to find some way in which Jesus had it much, much worse—even if only because he deserved none of it and we must admit that we probably deserve some small part of the misfortune that comes our way.

Mary's trials can serve to console us in that same upside-down sort of way. Many of us lose parents. Though some of us will aver that "my mother was a saint," Mary's mother, Anne, *was* a saint! Her father, Joachim, too! Her husband, Joseph, a man who stood by her side during the most trying of circumstances: a saint. Her Son, Jesus? 'Nuff said. Imagine the kindest, most selfless person you've known and then imagine that all the people closest to you in life were even more so. What must it be like to lose the company of such incredible people?

None of this minimizes our own sorrows, of course. Genghis Khan's mother probably loved her little boy every bit as much as Gandhi's mother loved him. But Mary and Jesus do show us that there is a way through such sorrows, even the most terrible sorrows.

The idea of life after death was not a given in the Jewish tradition. Scripture even mentions occasions when Jesus used differences of opinion on the matter (the Pharisees believed in an afterlife; the Sadducess did not) to spur lively debates. There is no question that Mary had profound faith. But her faith was missing some of the support that we take for granted. The Gospels had not yet been written. She may never have heard Jesus say, "I am the resurrection and the life," or any of his countless intimations at what would happen to him. We believe in the resurrection because Jesus rose from the dead. We have his assurance that those who die in the faith will also be raised. If Mary can demonstrate such profound faith without benefit of our experience of two thousand years of Christian teaching, we should be encouraged in our own.

This Christmas, celebrate the loved ones you still have in your life and allow yourself to believe that you will see all those you love again one day.

CHAPTER SEVEN

The Assumption and Coronation of Mary as Queen of Heaven

Hail, Holy Queen enthroned above, O Maria!
Hail, Mother of mercy and of love, O Maria!
Triumph all ye cherubim!
Sing with us ye seraphim!
Heaven and earth resound the hymn!
Salve, salve, salve, Regina!

Our life, our sweetness here below, O Maria!
Our hope in sorrow and in woe, O Maria!
Triumph all ye cherubim!
Sing with us ye seraphim!
Heaven and earth resound the hymn!
Salve, salve, salve, Regina!

And when our last breath leaves us, O Maria!
Show us thy son Christ Jesus, O Maria!
Triumph all ye cherubim!
Sing with us ye seraphim!

Heaven and earth resound the hymn!
Salve, salve, salve, Regina!

—*Salve Regina,* traditional hymn

*F*or centuries, Christians have debated the details of Mary's life. While most Protestant traditions tend to base their conclusions solely on what appears in Scripture, the Catholic Church values what we can learn from our rich tradition.

The names of St. Anne and St. Joachim do not appear in the Gospels, but they have been long held to be Mary's parents. The Bible does not record the death of St. Joseph, but tradition suggests that he died somewhere in that long silence between the finding in the temple and Jesus's public ministry. The reason he is venerated as the patron of a happy death is the understanding that he died in the arms of Jesus and Mary, quite literally.

Just so, it has long been the tradition in the Church that Mary was assumed into heaven. No one can see precisely when and where this happened (and there are varying opinions on the subject), but Pope Pius XII definitively ended all discussion of "if" with his apostolic constitution *Munificentissimus Deus*, which defined the Assumption as a dogma of the Church. In doing so, the pope spoke *ex cathedra*, an unusual move. So unusual, in fact, that the papacy has spoken in this way—the only time the doctrine of papal infallibility overtly comes into play—just twice in over two thousand years.

In doing so, Pius XII referred to the long tradition of the Church concerning this event. He said:

Christ's faithful, through the teaching and the leadership of their pastors, have learned from the sacred books that the Virgin Mary, throughout the course of her earthly pilgrimage, led a life troubled by cares, hardships, and sorrows, and that, moreover, what the holy old man Simeon had foretold actually came to pass, that is, that a terribly sharp sword pierced her heart as she stood under the cross of her divine Son, our Redeemer. In the same way, it was not difficult for them to admit that the great Mother of God, like her only begotten Son, had actually passed from this life. But this in no way prevented them from believing and from professing openly that her sacred body had never been subject to the corruption of the tomb, and that the august tabernacle of the Divine Word had never been reduced to dust and ashes. Actually, enlightened by divine grace and moved by affection for her, God's Mother and our own dearest Mother, they have contemplated in an ever clearer light the wonderful harmony and order of those privileges which the most provident God has lavished upon this loving associate of our Redeemer, privileges which reach such an exalted plane that, except for her, nothing created by God other than the human nature of Jesus Christ has ever reached this level. (14)

Essentially, Pius is telling us that Mary is something very special—something that the faithful have always known and believed. He works through all the ways she differs from the rest of humanity. He cites the writings of the great saints throughout the ages that have testified to Mary's Assumption. To highlight just a few:

St. Albert the Great wrote in his *Mariale*, "It is manifest that the most blessed Mother of God has been assumed above the choirs of angels. And this we believe in every way to be true."[3]

St. Bonaventure, in his sermon on the Assumption of the Blessed Virgin Mary, wrote, "We can see that she is there bodily...her blessedness would not have been complete unless she were there as a person. The soul is not a person, but the soul, joined to the body, is a person. It is manifest that she is there in soul and in body. Otherwise she would not possess her complete beatitude."[4]

St. Francis de Sales, in a sermon for the Feast of the Assumption asked, "What son would not bring his mother back to life and would not bring her into paradise after her death if he could?"[5]

I find Francis de Sales's appeal to what we can intuit of the relationship between Jesus and his Mother to be persuasive. Just as it seems right that he would visit her first upon his Resurrection, it seems right that he would bring her to himself at the end of her life.

Thus, the pope boldly declares:

> By the authority of our Lord Jesus Christ, of the Blessed Apostles Peter and Paul, and by our own authority, we pronounce, declare, and define it to be a divinely revealed dogma: that the Immaculate Mother of God, the ever Virgin Mary, having completed the course of her earthly life, was assumed body and soul into heavenly glory.
>
> Hence if anyone, which God forbid, should dare willfully to deny or to call into doubt that which we have defined, let him know that he has fallen away completely from the divine and Catholic Faith.[6]

An interesting point is the language Pius uses to describe the end of Mary's life. He does not say that she died and was resurrected, but he also doesn't say that she didn't die. The Greek Orthodox tradition celebrates a feast called the "dormition" (falling asleep) of Mary. Rather than defining as dogma something on which two ancient traditions differ, Pius used the phrase "having completed the course of her earthly life," which applies in either instance and respects both beliefs.

For the queenship of Mary, we do have witness from Scripture. Though the book of Revelation is notoriously slippery to interpret, the following verses are generally considered to be references to the Blessed Mother:

> A great portent appeared in heaven: a woman clothed with the sun, with the moon under her feet, and on her head a crown of twelve stars. (12:1)

> And she gave birth to a son, a male child, who is to rule all the nations with a rod of iron. (12:5)

Throughout the rest of this prophetic book, the emphasis is on the kingship of Christ. Since Mary is his Mother and here wears a crown, the title of Queen follows logically.

In his book, *100 Names of Mary: Stories and Prayers*, Anthony Chiffolo makes a strong case for our understanding of Mary as Queen of Heaven:

> Over the centuries the church fathers and mothers and theologians have made many references to Mary's queenship. Saint Alphonsus de' Liguori, for example, wrote, "We may thank our most loving Queen for all, since all comes to us from her hands and by her powerful intercession" (*The Glories of Mary*, II). The Litany of Loreto invokes the intercession of Mary as queen nine times, and...the final mystery of the rosary is a meditation on the coronation of the Blessed Virgin Mary—her crowning as queen. The concept has become so generally accepted that Pope Pius XII instituted the liturgical feast of the Queenship of Mary in 1954, issuing that same year an encyclical about Mary's queenship, *Ad Coeli Reginam*.
>
> Mary's queenship is one of love and service, in which she gives of herself for the good of humankind. Indeed, she gave her son, accepting his sacrifice for the salvation of all creation. For this gift—the ultimate gift a mother can bestow—God has crowned her Queen of the Universe.

Scripture paints a portrait of Mary as a woman of tremendous dignity, one who can handle the most extraordinary circumstances with quiet grace. To celebrate her coronation as Queen of Heaven seems to simply acknowledge the regal character she has always possessed.

Christmas can inspire us to be our very best and simultaneously exert pressures that make us our very worst. As Mary's example shows us, it is those stressful times that reveal to others (and us) what we're really made of. When you squeeze a lemon, you get lemon juice. That's not a result of the pressure put on the lemon— the juice was always what was inside. It just didn't show itself until the stress was on.

Rather than expecting the impossible of ourselves or trying to disguise what we're really made of, the best practice is to look deeply at who we are, where we've been, and where we're going. If we spend some time in prayer trying to see ourselves as God sees us, we'll have an accurate portrait of what we are—both the faults of the current moment, and the glorious potential we have as children of the Most High.

This Christmas, take some of the pressure off yourself. Acknowledge that the King and Queen of Heaven have things well in hand and will find a way to make this holy season—and you—very good. You just have to let them.

NOTES

1. *Liturgy of the Hours,* Office of Readings for December 20, from St. Bernard, Homily 4, 8–9.
2. *Thinking Faith,* Pope Pius XII, *Munificentissimus Deus,* 30.
3. *Munificentissimus Deus,* 32.
4. *Munificentissimus Deus,* 35.
5. *Munificentissimus Deus,* 44–45.

BIBLIOGRAPHY

Aquilina, Mike. *Angels of God: The Bible, the Church and the Heavenly Hosts* (Cincinnati: Servant, 2009).

Benedict XVI, Pope. *Mary: The Church at the Source* (San Francisco: Ignatius, 2005).

Cameron, Peter John. *Mysteries of the Virgin Mary: Living Our Lady's Graces* (Cincinnati: Servant, 2010).

Chiffolo, Anthony F. *100 Names of Mary: Stories and Prayers* (Cincinnati: St. Anthony Messenger Press, 2002).

Dupre, Judith. *Full of Grace: Encountering Mary in Faith, Art, and Life* (New York: Random House, 2010).

Habig, Marion A., ed. *Saint Francis of Assisi: Omnibus of Sources* (Cincinnati: St. Anthony Messenger Press, 2008).

John Paul II, Pope. *Rosarium Virginis Mariae.* Apostolic Letter. Available at www.vatican.va.

The Liturgy of the Hours (4 vols.) (Totowa, N.J.: Catholic Book, 1998).

Mahoney, Jack, S.J. "The Risen Jesus and His Mother," *Thinking Faith*, December 2011. Online journal of the British Jesuits available at www.thinkingfaith.org.

McBride, Alfred, O.PRAEM. *Images of Mary* (Cincinnati: St. Anthony Messenger Press, 1999).

Moyer, Ginny Kubitz. *Mary and Me: Catholic Women Reflect on the Mother of God* (Cincinnati: St. Anthony Messenger Press, 2008).

Pelikan, Jaroslav. *Mary Through the Centuries: Her Place in the History of Culture* (New Haven, Conn.: Yale University Press, 1998).

Pius XII, Pope. *Munificentissimus Deus.* Apostolic Constitution, November 1, 1950. Available at www.vatican.va.

Sri, Edward. *The New Rosary in Scripture: Biblical Insights for Praying the 20 Mysteries* (Cincinnati: Servant, 2003).

ABOUT THE AUTHOR

Kathleen M. Carroll is managing editor of the book department at Franciscan Media. She is the author of *St. Francis: A Short Biography*, *A Franciscan Christmas*, *A Catholic Christmas*, and *Keeping the Faith in Ohio: Words of Hope and Comfort from Our Spiritual Leaders*.